44 Days:

the rise & fall
of a doomed romance

JENNIFER DOAN

ISBN: 9798873403875

DEDICATION

I suppose it's dedicated to you
even if I wish it wasn't
even if I hope you never
touch these pages

I wrote the first poem in this series the night of our first date. As things progressed, I continued to write and it became a piece of living art.

Each poem was written as it was felt and at times that makes this creation a little embarrassing to look back on. But the hope is that it speaks to anyone who also falls for people too hard and too fast, with no regard for their own heart.

You are a beautiful, sensitive soul and you deserve all the compassion that you pour into others.

#1 FIRST DATE SPOILERS

He took a drag on his vape immediately before he caught my eye and clumsily blew the smoke away, quickly pulling me into an excited embrace

Maybe our timing was destined to be off

#2 WRITER'S AMIRIGHT?

I knew I was going to like you.

There was something in the way you wrote.

Straight from brain to page.

#3

Every morning I'm jolted awake

by the urge to know what you're thinking

#4

Suddenly poetry makes sense again

#5 BROKEN RECORD

Everyday it's you

and it's you

and it's you

and it's you

#6 SPEECHLESS

the ways I want you require words beyond comprehension

but I'd be remiss not to mention the way your hair falls in your face and you breathe deep as I brush the strands away and when your eyes move to the left as you think walking me to the brink of insanity as I can hardly contain any modicum of decency when I read the wall of text you use to describe what we could be and how you see me and I know it's so soon and any sane human would prescribe apprehension adding a new dimension to what I thought I had the capacity to feel and whether or not it ends up being real isn't of concern to me now I'd rather bask in the glow of potential than get too self-referential to the poems where I've been burned before because

we're here

and it's magic

and I've hardly touched the ground

I'll get around to telling you as soon as I can speak again

#7 WRITERS, AMIRIGHT? II

I would break your heart

for the privilege of reading

the words you would use

to slander me.

That's how good you are.

#8

And then I think he ran out of energy for me

#9

Maybe it's nothing.

Maybe it never was.

#10

I can't write without

the fear of you reading it.

Or maybe that you never will.

#11

One carefully queued compliment

and it breaks me back into your orbit

#12 WHAT'S UNDER THERE?

17

Sometimes it's like reaching

through a thick fog

just for a moment

of recognition

If it lifted would you still look the same

Or am I compelled by the mist

#13

I told you I wanted someone

to love you properly.

I didn't tell you I wanted it to be me.

#14 WRITER'S, AMIRIGHT? III

Nothing felt more natural than

falling for you

through the words

you wrote

for other women

#15

What I wouldn't give

to kiss the man you were

before someone taught you

that love isn't worth

the insanity

#16

Loving you is a secret I keep

not because I fear your response

or I think it's too soon

But because I'm not sure if

your heart has the capacity

to love me and break at the same time

#17

you're gone again

and I'm left grasping

at a man shaped hole

cleaved in empty air

it's thick with silence

but I can't dig my fingers in

#18 CRAFT NIGHT

With all the extra thread

from being strung along

I could weave a noose

and hang our love from the rafters

#19 MAYBE WE SHOULD HAVE WAITED TO HAVE THIS CONVERSATION

They say you shouldn't make big decisions

on a full moon

Yet here we are

dissipating into nothingness

like smoke from your lips

or my resolve under the pressure of our last kiss

but I couldn't bear to part with whatever time

I could pry from your broken heart

was it selfish of me

or maybe you

or was it worth it to be blinded by

what little light you had left

neither of us have fingers left to point

so we sit in dead air

and if the moon had any opinions on the matter

she kept them to herself

#20 I'LL TAKE TWO

I asked what he could give me

and he said "nothing"

Somehow it still sounded like a good deal

#21 I'M NOT BUYING IT

I convince myself that I could sit

in a room with you and not care

That I could watch your hair fall in that way

and not be launched directly

out of my body

That we could lay platonically in your bed

staring at stars on the ceiling,

talking about everything

but our broken hearts and

I wouldn't try to press my palm into yours

I assure myself that

watching your forehead crease

as you speak wouldn't

eviscerate me completely and

the smell of your chest

in a restrained embrace wouldn't

plunge me firmly into madness

That every word that dripped from your lips

wouldn't drive me to

build an altar to your mind

That every thought you shared wouldn't

melt down the back of my spine and

I'd catch my confessions before they whipped abruptly from
my throat

In this moment, I'm convinced I could stand in your doorway
and feel nothing.

We would laugh

No one would cry

We would be fine

(I'm not sure how I convince myself of that)

#22

I reread every word we wrote

to each other

and wonder how

I wasn't supposed to fall

a man on an app asks

what I'm passionate about lately

the first thing that comes to mind is

    crying

#23

I'm fine until it gets dark

and it seems like it's always dark

#24 JEALOUS

And yet, when you sit down to think about

what hurts the most

I wouldn't even crack your top ten

#25 YOU'VE BEEN SUPERLIKED

You let one of the notifications take you out

and spend the evening being

"special"

"funny"

and "gorgeous"

but it's not enough

They don't crack you open

toss the veneer,

peer inside and say

"this is what you were hiding?

this is better than all of it"

so you go home and scroll and swipe

like you're digging for some unearthed truth

and you wonder if anyone will ever see you

so briefly and beautifully ever again

when your phone bloops with a "hey gorgeous"

you respond almost immediately

#26

Maybe it wasn't love

but it could have been

and that's much more interesting

#27

That gritty, unpalatable energy.

The moment you smell it on me it's over.

The thick scent of the unchosen.

It doesn't matter how much

you were enamoured before

As soon as they confront you

soaked in need

grasping at your heels

mewling for scraps of affection

those feelings dissolve.

as soon as I felt it

we were done for

#28

you filled me to the brim

then shook the bottle

it's not my fault if your shoes got wet

#29

I believe you when you speak

do you?

#30 HEIST

I know it was brief

I know I barely knew you

But what I knew fit so perfectly into my frame

I wanted more than you had.

She took it all with her when she left

and though I tried to pry it from her hands

they stayed frozen stiff

around your throat

and as you gasped for air,

you looked at me like art

stuck behind a pane of glass

beautifully unattainable

but useless if you can't breathe.

So you breathe instead.

and the light goes out

and the tourists are gone

and my air sits ragged in my chest

heaving in a translucent box

She robbed us.

and I'll never know her face

but I can't forgive her for that.

#31 I'M ONLY KIND OF JOKING

The only cure for a shredded love

is to cut it clean from the bone

age it in a smoke filled room

and dry it into a chewy jerky

that absolutely no one can enjoy

#32

if I let go

what would I do all day?

#33

it's calm again

and if you don't show up by spring

that's ok too

I'm planting myself deep and seeing who

surfaces when I breach the soil

#34

And if you come to me again

heart mended

will you still shine as bright as the

idol I've woven into words

will our undoing be my need to

see you through embossed lettering

not one crease enclosed from cover to cover

will there be pages to lay your pen to

if I've already played our parts to completion

exercising an artist's right to embellish the beauty

are the words better than we ever were

and then again, shouldn't they be?

#35

We can't bear to look

each other in the eye

so we come together as poets

It's easier to breathe your words

than the air in your between your sheets

the place where you praised my skin and

I swore to never misplace the privilege

of your hands on my thighs

For now, we're only poets

who once carefully removed

each other's clothes

and made no promises

who had no elegant words

for the way we used to melt

after mere hours

of pointless conversation

who's fumbling hands in low light

knew no prose

only the languid urgency

of pressure and release

the page is a much safer place

to love you

so we speak as poets do

distanced

pretentious

and yearning

#36

my words reach you like starlight;

captivating

but a hundred years too late

#37

the sky is bright

in the way where light

bounces off the grey

casting a bland glow

to match the memories

I suppose

#38 MY SHIFT ENDS AT 5

sitting in the backroom

between wanting

and exhaustion

the fluorescent light

really brings out your features

I hadn't noticed how

stale the coffee is

until now

I wince with every sip

but drink my mug dry

#39 FOR JUST SOME GUY

In hindsight, 44 poems is a bit much

#40

was it the limerence?

does it matter?

I can spend my day

diagnosing my mind

or I can concede that

my experience is mine

regardless of the reasoning

#41

as easy as it might be

not to,

I refuse to give us both

anything less than

grace

humanity

and forgiveness

when our trauma

spoke louder

than truth

#42

One day

it stopped being a fantasy

or a tragedy

just

two people

attempting to pass

something fleeting

from palm to palm

leaking a little light

with each exchange

But with hands hesitantly cupped

they cradled hope

for one exquisite moment

And I'm so proud of them for even trying

#43 ALMOST OVER

Once you've cried and you've agonized and you've let the panic drain from your veins,

there's just a stillness.

A sadness with rounded edges.

The problem becomes that we never went deep enough to hate or love each other. So a gooey ball of potential sits on the slab, but there's no one around who cares enough to carve it into anything.

All the commotion and crushing intensity of wanting someone who wants you back has nowhere to go.

There's no rage to funnel it into.

There's no cataclysmic event.

I'd call it bad timing, but so rarely does such a thing correct itself that it feels more apt to consider it a soft ending.

It's not as tumultuous and it's easier to get over. But it really is just too fucking bad.

Though, if our entire purpose was to hold each other while fall transitioned into winter, I suppose there are worse ways to watch the temperature drop.

And if that really is all it will ever be, then I'll recall you sad & beautiful with a deep capacity for joy and a mind I could bathe in.

And you'll hold that high status until shown otherwise. Because that is the heartbreaking upside to never truly knowing one another...

We get to be so immutably flawless.

#44

this isn't a poem

just a note to say

I'm saving this spot

for if we ever

get our timing right

ABOUT THE AUTHOR

Jennifer is a queer artist, performer and writer living in Vancouver, BC.

They believe in the power of rhythm, expression, mouth feel and creating absolutely terrible, bad, no-good art.

Give them something to cringe about.

You can follow Jenn's poetry account on instagram @somethingtocringeabout

www.ingramcontent.com/pod-product-compliance
Lightning Source LLC
Chambersburg PA
CBHW071617270726
48661CB00014BA/2565